THE MEN'S HYGIENE HANDBOOK

Guide to Eliminating Body and Foot Odor While Smelling Great

Corey S. Mayle

COPYRIGHT PAGE

All rights reserved. No part of this publication may be republished in any form or by any means, including photocopying, scanning, or otherwise without prior written permission from the copyright holder.

Copyright © 2023 Corey S. Mayle

Medical Disclaimer

The information provided in this handbook is for educational purposes only and is not intended to be a substitute for medical advice. It is important to seek the advice of your healthcare provider if you have any serious health concerns before trying any remedies. Please note that the information or products mentioned in this handbook have not been evaluated by the Food and Drug Administration (FDA). This information is not intended to diagnose, treat, cure, or prevent any medical condition.

INTRODUCTION 10

CHAPTER 1 14

ORAL HEALTH 14

Importance of Good Oral Hygiene 14

Brush Your Teeth Regularly 17

Floss Daily 19

Make Use of Mouthwash 19

Limit Intake of Sugary and Acidic Foods 20

Stay Hydrated By Drinking Plenty of Water 21

Pay Regular Visits to the Dentist's Office 21

Quit Smoking 22

CHAPTER 2 24

MEN'S HAIR HEALTH 24

How Much Washing Does Your Hair Require 24

Condition Hair 26

Protect Your Hair from Heat 26

Trim Hair Regularly 26

Avoid Harsh Chemicals 27

Protect from the sun 27

CHAPTER 3 28

EAR CARE 28

Keep Your Ears Clean 28

Protect Your Ears from Loud Noises 28

Avoid Inserting Foreign Objects into Your Ears 29

Dry Your Ears after Swimming or Showering 29

Check for Earwax Buildup 29

Monitor for Hearing Loss 30

CHAPTER 4 31

NAILS CARE 31

Keep Them Clean 31

Trim Regularly 31

Moisturize 32

Avoid Biting or Picking 32

Protect From Harsh Chemicals 32

The Men's Hygiene Handbook | 5

Check for Signs of Infection 33

CHAPTER 5 34

SKINCARE 34

Cleanse Regularly 34

Exfoliate 34

Moisturize 35

Protect From the Sun 35

Shave Carefully 35

Watch Your Diet 36

CHAPTER 6 37

THE MANLY BEARDS 37

Wash Regularly 37

Condition 37

Comb and Brush 38

Trim Regularly 38

Moisturize 38

Be Patient 38

CHAPTER 7 40

PUBIC HAIRS 40

Trim 40

Cleanse 40

Moisturize 41

Wear Breathable Clothing 41

Avoid Harsh Chemicals 41

Be Careful When Shaving 41

Consider Professional Grooming 42

CHAPTER 8 43

CLOTHES AND UNDERWEARS 43

Read Care Labels 43

Sort Your Laundry 43

Use the Right Detergent 44

Wash In Cold Water 44

Dry Properly 44

Store Properly 44

Replace Regularly 45

CHAPTER 9 46

SMELLY FEET 46

Wash Your Feet Daily 46

Wear Breathable Shoes 46

Wear Clean Socks 47

Use Foot Powder 47

Soak Your Feet 47

Keep Toenails Trimmed 47

Don't Share Shoes or Socks 48

CHAPTER 10 49

STRONG BODY ODOR 49

Curbing the Menace 52

Shower Regularly 52

Wear Breathable Clothing 52

Wash Clothes Regularly 53

Change Clothes after Exercising 53

Watch Your Diet 53

Stay Hydrated 53

Use Isopropyl Alcohol..54

Clean the Underarm Area..54

Dry the Underarm Area...54

Apply Isopropyl Alcohol..55

Allow the Alcohol to Dry..55

Reapply As Necessary..55

Use Organic Coconut Oil...56

INTRODUCTION

The Men's Hygiene Handbook is your ultimate guide to all things hygiene for men. Good personal hygiene is essential not only for your health and well-being but also for your confidence and self-esteem. Whether you're a busy professional, an athlete, or just someone who wants to look and feel your best, this book has got you covered.

From grooming tips for your hair, nails, and skin, to advice on keeping your clothes and underwear fresh and clean, this book is packed with practical advice and useful tips to help you take care of your body and look your best. We'll cover topics like how to maintain a healthy beard, how to care for your pubic hair, and how to prevent common skin problems.

In this handbook, we also delved into how to deal with underarms and foot odor, which is also applicable to women. Underarm and foot odors can be incredibly embarrassing and frustrating issues to deal with. The social stigma associated with body odor can negatively impact one's self-confidence and make it challenging to interact with others. Even if you shower regularly and apply deodorant, it can feel like the odor is impossible to eliminate. This can lead to a vicious cycle of trying different products and remedies that only provide temporary relief.

However, the good news is that there is a permanent solution to this problem. By understanding the root cause of underarm and foot odor and taking proactive steps to address it, you can finally experience the freedom of being odor-free for life. This means no more feeling self-conscious or avoiding social situations.

Instead of wasting money on expensive products that don't work, it's important to take a holistic approach to tackle the root cause of the odor. In doing so, you can take control of your life and enjoy a newfound sense of confidence and freedom. In this handbook, we will explore the causes of underarm and foot odor and provide actionable tips to eliminate the problem once and for all.

This book is perfect for men of all ages and lifestyles, whether you're a seasoned hygiene pro or just starting to develop good hygiene habits. We believe that good hygiene is not only important for your physical health but also for your mental and emotional well-being. So let's dive in and discover the secrets to maintaining great hygiene and feeling confident every day.

Chapter 1
ORAL HEALTH

Oral health refers to the overall health of the mouth, including teeth, gums, and tongue. It is essential to maintain good oral hygiene practices, such as brushing teeth twice a day, flossing daily, and regularly visiting the dentist for check-ups and cleanings. Neglecting oral health can lead to various dental problems, such as cavities, gum disease, bad breath, and tooth loss.

Moreover, research has also found a link between poor oral health and other health conditions, such as heart disease, stroke, and diabetes. Thus, taking care of your oral health is crucial not only for your teeth and gums but also for your overall well-being.

Importance of Good Oral Hygiene

Oral health is an integral part of overall human wellness. In many ways, maintaining excellent dental health influences your overall well-being and quality of life.

- A healthy mouth allows you to enjoy your meals more, chew more effectively, consume healthier foods, keep your breath fresh, and prevent discomfort and tooth loss.
- It may have an impact on your physical and emotional health, as well as your financial and social life.
- Oral diseases may be unpleasant and irritating, and they can lead to additional issues.
- Most oral health disorders are preventable and treatable if detected early. If oral health concerns are not detected early, they may be costly to cure, and treatments can become more difficult and invasive.

- Many studies have revealed a correlation between poor dental health and other areas of the body's health.
- Diabetes, heart disease, pulmonary (lung) problems, some malignancies, pre-term birth, and even Alzheimer's disease are among these disorders.
- Many studies have also shown a link between gum disease (also known as periodontal disease) and illnesses such as diabetes, heart disease, pregnancy-related complications, and dementia. The precise relationship between these disorders and gum disease is unknown.

Here are some tips for men on how to care for their teeth and gums:

Brush Your Teeth Regularly

Brush your teeth twice daily for two minutes minimum each time with ~~fluoride~~ toothpaste. The American Dental Association recommends this.

Brushing helps dislodge food and plaque from between your teeth. Plaque is a white, sticky film that accumulates on the teeth. Plaque contains microorganisms. After eating a sugary meal or snack, bacteria in plaque produce acids that destroy tooth enamel. The strong outer layer that protects your teeth is called enamel.

The acid erodes tooth enamel over time. Cavities may result from this. Plaque that remains on the teeth develops into tartar. When you have tartar on your teeth, it is more difficult to keep them clean. Tartar accumulation on the gums also promotes inflammation, contributing to gum disease.

To preserve your teeth, avoid brushing them immediately after eating or drinking acidic foods or beverages. Soft drinks, such as soda and sports drinks, sour candies, citrus juices, and citrus fruits are all examples. The acid in them has the potential to soften the enamel. Brushing your teeth too soon after eating or drinking anything acidic will wear away the enamel. Brush after an hour. During this period, your saliva washes away the acid, and your enamel hardens once again.

If you have arthritis, have difficulty gripping a toothbrush, or wear braces, consider using an electric or battery-powered toothbrush. Those toothbrushes may be more user-friendly.

Additionally, it is essential to replace your toothbrush every three to four months, or earlier if the bristles start to wear out. Adhering to this straightforward oral care routine can promote a healthier mouth and help prevent dental complications.

Floss Daily

Dental floss is an essential item for oral and dental health, and it should be used at least once a day. Dental floss, which is essential for avoiding tooth decay and gum disease, also helps to prevent dental plaque.

Flossing is the process of using dental floss to remove plaque and food particles that are stuck between your teeth. Ensure that you floss your teeth a minimum of once per day.

Make Use of Mouthwash

The utilization of mouthwash can aid in eliminating bacteria and enhancing the freshness of your breath. Choose a mouthwash that's alcohol-free and has fluoride.

Limit Intake of Sugary and Acidic Foods

Consuming foods that are high in sugar and acidity can increase the likelihood of developing tooth decay and gum disease. Thus, it is advisable to regulate your intake of such foods to mitigate the risk of dental problems.

It is important to note that a diet that is high in sugar and acidic substances can result in the erosion of tooth enamel, making teeth more susceptible to decay and other oral issues. Therefore, opting for a balanced diet that includes fresh fruits, vegetables, and dairy products can promote optimal oral health.

Stay Hydrated By Drinking Plenty of Water

Consuming water can assist in rinsing away food particles and bacteria present in your mouth. It is recommended to aim for a minimum of eight glasses of water per day.

Pay Regular Visits to the Dentist's Office

To ensure optimal oral health, it is imperative to schedule regular dental check-ups and cleanings. Experts recommend visiting your dentist a minimum of two times a year to keep your teeth and gums in good condition. These routine appointments allow your dentist to identify and address any potential dental issues promptly.

During a dental cleaning, the dental hygienist removes plaque and tartar buildup, which can lead to tooth decay and gum disease if not adequately addressed. Regular dental check-ups can help detect and treat dental problems early, preventing more severe dental issues from developing. Therefore, making regular dental visits a priority is vital for maintaining good oral health.

Quit Smoking

Smoking can cause tooth staining, gum disease, and oral cancer. Cessation of smoking is considered among the most beneficial actions you can take to improve both your oral health and overall well-being.

Incorporating these suggestions into your routine can help maintain healthy teeth and gums and prevent dental complications. It is crucial to bear in mind that good oral health is a fundamental aspect of overall health and well-being. Therefore, taking care of your teeth and gums is vital.

By adhering to a regular oral care routine, such as brushing and flossing regularly, scheduling dental check-ups and cleanings, and regulating your intake of sugary and acidic foods, you can promote good oral health and a bright smile. So, remember to prioritize your oral health to enhance your overall health and well-being.

Chapter 2
MEN'S HAIR HEALTH

Investing in a healthy head of hair is worthwhile. Finally, it means you'll shed less, suffer less thinning or hairline recession, have less breakage and split ends, and even keep your hair's thickness and volume. Taking exceptional care of your hair from the scalp out means you are having fantastic hair days more often. This is either because you're investing in the right products or because your doctor has prescribed a specific prescription. Maintaining good hygiene is crucial for healthy hair, and this is true for men's hair as well. Here are some tips for caring for men's hair:

How Much Washing Does Your Hair Require

Taking daily showers is encouraged to maintain good hygiene as a man, but washing your hair regularly might be murder. Baths daily may also dry out your skin and deplete it of the natural oils it needs to appear healthy. It is good to apply a good moisturizer to replenish your skin. While certain men's occupations need daily showers, caution should be taken on how often you wash your hair.

Instead, doctors recommend washing no more than three times each week, unless your scalp is very greasy or you've sweated much that day. Over washing, including vigorous washing may injure your scalp and hair. It makes your hair dull and brittle, as well as dry, which means it breaks more readily and is more difficult to manage. You may want to wash your hair more often because it is dry, but the reverse is true. Instead of washing your hair more often to maintain it healthy and preserve its natural oils, you should wash it less frequently.

Condition Hair

After shampooing, it's important to use a conditioner to replenish the hair's natural oils and keep it moisturized. Apply the conditioner evenly from the mid-lengths to the ends of the hair, and leave it in for a few minutes before rinsing.

Protect Your Hair from Heat

Excessive heat can damage the hair, so avoid using hot styling tools like blow dryers or flat irons daily. If you do use these tools, use a heat protectant spray to minimize damage.

Trim Hair Regularly

Getting regular haircuts or trims is important to maintain healthy hair. Trimming the ends of the hair regularly helps prevent split ends and breakage.

Avoid Harsh Chemicals

Avoid using harsh chemicals like bleach or hair dyes, as they can damage the hair and scalp. If you do use these products, be sure to follow the instructions carefully and use them sparingly.

Protect from the sun

Protect your hair from the sun's harmful rays by wearing a hat or using a protective spray or serum that contains SPF.

In addition to these tips, it's important to maintain a healthy diet and lifestyle to promote healthy hair growth. Eating a balanced diet rich in vitamins and minerals, staying hydrated, and reducing stress can all help improve the health of your hair.

Chapter 3
EAR CARE

The human ear is a very sensitive organ. Its primary function is to detect, transmit, and transduce sound. Another crucial function of the human ear is to maintain a feeling of equilibrium. Taking care of your ears is an important part of maintaining good overall health. Here are some tips for men on how to care for their ears:

Keep Your Ears Clean

Clean your ears regularly with a damp cloth or cotton swab. Be gentle and avoid inserting anything too deep into your ear canal, as this can damage your eardrum.

Protect Your Ears from Loud Noises

Exposure to loud noises can damage your hearing over time. Wear earplugs or earmuffs when exposed to loud noises, such as at concerts or construction sites.

Avoid Inserting Foreign Objects into Your Ears

Avoid inserting anything into your ears, such as cotton swabs, bobby pins, or pens. These objects can damage your ear canal or eardrum.

Dry Your Ears after Swimming or Showering

Water that remains in your ears after swimming or showering can cause ear infections. Use a towel to dry your ears thoroughly.

Check for Earwax Buildup

Excessive earwax can cause hearing problems or infections. If you notice a buildup of earwax, consult with a healthcare professional to have it removed safely.

Monitor for Hearing Loss

Pay attention to changes in your hearing and seek medical attention if you notice any hearing loss or ringing in your ears.

By following these tips, you can maintain good ear health and prevent hearing problems. If you experience any ear pain, discharge from your ear, or hearing problems, consult with a healthcare professional (usually an ENT specialist) for proper evaluation and treatment.

Chapter 4
NAILS CARE

Taking good care of nails is important for both men and women, as it promotes good hygiene and helps prevent infections. Here are some tips for men on how to care for their nails:

Keep Them Clean

Regularly cleaning your nails is an important step in nail care. Use a nail brush and soap to gently clean under your nails, and be sure to dry them thoroughly afterward to prevent bacteria growth.

Trim Regularly

Keeping nails trimmed and neat is important for both hygiene and aesthetics. Use a nail clipper to trim nails straight across, and use a file to smooth any rough edges.

Moisturize

Keeping nails and cuticles moisturized can help prevent dryness and cracking. Use a hand lotion or cuticle cream to moisturize the area around the nails, and massage it gently to promote circulation.

Avoid Biting or Picking

Biting or picking at nails can damage the nail bed and increase the risk of infection. If you have a habit of biting your nails, try using bitter-tasting nail polish to discourage the behavior.

Protect From Harsh Chemicals

Exposure to harsh chemicals like cleaning products or solvents can damage nails and make them brittle. Wear gloves when handling these substances to protect your nails.

Check for Signs of Infection

Regularly checking your nails for signs of infection, such as redness or swelling, can help catch any issues early on. In case you observe any indications of infection, promptly seek medical assistance.

In addition to these tips, maintaining a healthy diet and lifestyle can also promote healthy nails. Eating a balanced diet rich in vitamins and minerals, staying hydrated, and avoiding smoking can all help improve the health of your nails.

Chapter 5
SKINCARE

Caring for your skin is an important part of overall hygiene, and it's not just for women. Men should also take care of their skin to promote healthy and youthful-looking skin. Here are some tips for men on how to care for their skin:

Cleanse Regularly

It's important to cleanse your skin regularly to remove dirt, oil, and impurities that can clog pores and cause acne. Use a gentle cleanser twice a day, morning and night, and avoid using hot water, which can strip the skin of its natural oils.

Exfoliate

Exfoliating helps remove dead skin cells and promote cell turnover, revealing fresh, healthy skin. Use a gentle scrub or exfoliating tool once or twice a week, and avoid over-exfoliating, which can damage the skin.

Moisturize

Keeping the skin moisturized is crucial for maintaining its hydration and overall health. Choose a moisturizer that suits your skin type, and apply it twice a day, after cleansing and before bed.

Protect From the Sun

Protecting your skin from the sun's harmful UV rays is crucial for preventing skin damage and premature aging. Use a broad-spectrum sunscreen with SPF 30 or higher, and reapply every two hours if you're outdoors for an extended time.

Shave Carefully

Shaving can irritate the skin and cause razor burns, so it's important to shave carefully. Use a sharp razor to shave in the direction of hair growth, and avoid shaving over the same area multiple times.

Watch Your Diet

Eating a healthy diet that's rich in vitamins and minerals can help improve the health of your skin. Consuming foods that are rich in antioxidants, such as fruits and vegetables, can aid in safeguarding the skin against damage.

In addition to these tips, staying hydrated, getting enough sleep, and reducing stress can also help improve the health of your skin.

Chapter 6
THE MANLY BEARDS

Beards can be a stylish and attractive addition to a man's appearance, but they do require some maintenance to keep them looking their best. Here are some tips for men on how to care for their beards:

Wash Regularly

Just like the hair on your head, your beard can get dirty and greasy. Wash your beard regularly with a gentle shampoo to keep it clean and fresh.

Condition

Using a beard conditioner can help keep your beard soft and manageable. Apply the conditioner after washing your beard, and let it sit for a few minutes before rinsing it out.

Comb and Brush

Combing and brushing your beard can help keep it tidy and prevent tangling. Use a beard comb or brush to gently detangle your beard, starting at the bottom and working your way up.

Trim Regularly

Regularly trimming your beard can assist in maintaining a neat appearance. Use beard scissors or clippers to trim the ends of your beard, and use a trimmer to shape it to your desired style.

Moisturize

Just like the skin on your face, the skin under your beard can get dry and itchy. Use a beard oil or balm to moisturize the skin under your beard and keep it hydrated.

Be Patient

Growing a beard takes time, so be patient and resist the urge to trim or style it too soon. Give your beard at least a month to grow in fully before deciding on a style or trimming it.

In addition to these tips, maintaining a healthy diet and lifestyle can also promote healthy beard growth. Eating a balanced diet rich in vitamins and minerals, staying hydrated, and getting enough sleep can all help improve the health of your beard.

Chapter 7
PUBIC HAIRS

Caring for your pubic hair is an important part of overall hygiene for men, and it can also help prevent irritation and infection. Here are some tips for men on how to care for their pubic hair:

Trim

Trimming your pubic hair can help keep it neat, and prevent it from getting too long and tangled. Use scissors or clippers to trim your hair, and be careful not to cut yourself.

Cleanse

Keeping your pubic area clean is important to prevent bacterial and fungal infections. Use a gentle cleanser to wash your pubic area daily, and make sure to rinse thoroughly.

Moisturize

Moisturizing your pubic area can help prevent dryness and itching. Use a moisturizing lotion or oil after cleansing to keep the skin hydrated.

Wear Breathable Clothing

Wearing tight clothing can trap moisture and heat, which can lead to irritation and infection. Wear loose-fitting, breathable clothing to allow air to circulate and prevent sweat from building up.

Avoid Harsh Chemicals

Avoid using harsh chemicals, such as hair removal creams, on your pubic area. These can cause irritation and inflammation.

Be Careful When Shaving

If you choose to shave your pubic hair, be careful not to cut yourself. Use a sharp razor to shave in the direction of hair growth, and avoid going over the same area multiple times.

Consider Professional Grooming

If you're uncomfortable grooming your pubic hair yourself, consider getting professional grooming services at a salon or spa.

Remember, every person's pubic hair is different, and there's no one-size-fits-all approach to grooming. Find what works best for you and your preferences, and always prioritize hygiene and safety when caring for your pubic hair.

Chapter 8
CLOTHES AND UNDERWEARS

Keeping your clothes and underwear clean and well-maintained is essential for maintaining good hygiene and extending the lifespan of your garments. Here are some tips for men on how to care for their clothes and underwear:

Read Care Labels

Every garment comes with a care label that includes specific instructions for washing and caring for the item. Make sure to read and follow these instructions carefully to avoid damaging your clothes.

Sort Your Laundry

Separate your laundry into different piles based on color and fabric type. Wash whites separately from darks, and avoid washing delicate fabrics with rougher fabrics that can cause damage.

Use the Right Detergent

Choose a laundry detergent that's appropriate for your fabric type and washing machine. Avoid using too much detergent, as this can leave a residue on your clothes and cause irritation.

Wash In Cold Water

Using cold water to wash your clothes can help prevent fading and shrinkage. It can also save energy and money on your utility bills.

Dry Properly

Avoid over-drying your clothes and underwear, as this can cause shrinkage and damage to the fabric. Follow care label instructions for drying, and consider air-drying delicate fabrics to prevent damage.

Store Properly

Store your clothes and underwear in a clean, dry, and well-ventilated area to prevent mustiness and mildew. Avoid hanging knits and sweaters, as this can cause stretching and misshaping.

Replace Regularly

Clothes and underwear wear out over time, so it's important to replace them regularly. Discard items that are ripped, torn, or stained, and replace them with new ones.

Remember, taking good care of your clothes and underwear not only helps you look and feel your best but also saves you money in the long run by extending the lifespan of your garments. By following these tips, you can maintain your clothes and underwear in great condition and ensure that they last as long as possible.

Chapter 9
SMELLY FEET

Smelly feet can be embarrassing and uncomfortable, but there are steps you can take to keep your feet smelling fresh and clean. Here are some tips for men on how to care for their smelly feet:

Wash Your Feet Daily

Make sure to wash your feet with soap and water every day, especially after exercising or sweating. Make sure to dry them completely, including the areas between your toes.

Wear Breathable Shoes

Choose shoes made from breathable materials like leather or canvas, and avoid shoes made from synthetic materials. Also, make sure your shoes fit properly to allow for good air circulation.

Wear Clean Socks

Change your socks daily or more often if you have sweaty feet. Opt for socks crafted from breathable fabrics such as cotton or wool.

Use Foot Powder

Apply foot powder or cornstarch to your feet to absorb moisture and reduce odor. You can also sprinkle some inside your shoes.

Soak Your Feet

Soaking your feet in warm water with Epsom salt or apple cider vinegar can help reduce odor and soothe tired feet.

Keep Toenails Trimmed

Trim your toenails regularly and make sure to clean under them to prevent bacteria from accumulating.

Don't Share Shoes or Socks

Sharing shoes or socks can spread bacteria and fungi that cause foot odor and infections.

By following these tips, you can keep your feet smelling fresh and clean. Remember, good foot hygiene is important not only for your comfort but also for your overall health and well-being. If you have persistent foot odor or other foot problems, consult with a healthcare professional.

Chapter 10
STRONG BODY ODOR

Body odor is a result of the combination of bacteria and sweat on the skin. The smell can vary depending on factors such as hormones, diet, infections, medications, or underlying conditions like diabetes. Prescription-strength antiperspirants or medications may help manage body odor.

When sweat comes into contact with bacteria on the skin, it creates body odor. The odor can have different characteristics, such as being sweet, sour, tangy, or resembling onions. The amount of sweat doesn't necessarily determine body odor. Some individuals may have an unpleasant odor without excessive sweating, while others may sweat heavily without a noticeable smell. This is because body odor is influenced by the type of bacteria on the skin and how it interacts with sweat, rather than the sweat itself.

Sweating is a natural process regulated by two types of sweat glands: eccrine and apocrine. Eccrine glands secrete sweat directly onto the skin's surface, which helps cool the body. This sweat doesn't have a smell. Apocrine glands which are found in areas like the armpits and groin, release sweat into hair follicles. When this sweat mixes with bacteria on the skin, it can produce an odor. Apocrine glands become active during puberty, explaining why body odor typically starts during adolescence.

While sweating is a normal bodily function, certain factors can contribute to unpleasant body odor. These include specific foods, hygiene practices, genetics, and conditions like hyperhidrosis, which causes excessive sweating. Changes in sweat production or odor can indicate underlying medical conditions.

Men and people assigned male at birth tend to experience body odor more frequently due to having more apocrine glands as a result of increased hair growth. Body odor typically begins at puberty.

Various factors can affect body odor, including exercise, stress, hot weather, being overweight, and genetics. Medications, supplements, and certain foods can also contribute to bad-smelling sweat. Conditions such as diabetes, gout, menopause, overactive thyroid, liver disease, kidney disease, and infectious diseases can lead to changes in body odor.

Hormonal changes can influence body odor, such as during menopause when hot flashes and night sweats occur. Fluctuations in hormones during menstruation or pregnancy may also alter body odor. Research suggests that body odor changes during ovulation to attract potential mates.

Certain foods rich in sulfur, like onions, garlic, cabbage, broccoli, and red meat, can contribute to body odor. Sulfur, which smells like rotten eggs, can be released in sweat, resulting in an unpleasant smell. Other dietary triggers include monosodium glutamate (MSG), caffeine, spices like curry or cumin, hot sauce, and alcohol. Reducing or eliminating these triggers from the diet may help improve body odor.

Curbing the Menace

Strong body odor can be a nuisance and make you self-conscious, but there are steps you can take to control it. Here are some tips for men on how to care for their strong body odor:

Shower Regularly

Shower at least once a day with soap and warm water. This helps remove sweat and bacteria that can cause body odor.

Wear Breathable Clothing

Choose clothes made from breathable fabrics like cotton or wool. Avoid synthetic fabrics that trap sweat and bacteria.

Wash Clothes Regularly

Wash your clothes regularly, especially those that come into contact with sweat. This helps remove bacteria and odors.

Change Clothes after Exercising

Change out of sweaty clothes immediately after exercising. This helps prevent bacteria from accumulating on your skin and clothing.

Watch Your Diet

Certain foods like garlic, onions, and spicy foods can cause strong body odor. It's advisable to steer clear of these foods or restrict your consumption of them

Stay Hydrated

Drinking plenty of water helps flush out toxins and reduce body odor.

Use Isopropyl Alcohol

Isopropyl alcohol is an effective solution for eliminating body odor that may emanate from the underarms of a man. The odor is usually caused by the presence of bacteria on the skin that feed on sweat and produce an unpleasant smell.

Here are the steps on how to apply isopropyl alcohol to get rid of the odor:

Clean the Underarm Area

Before applying isopropyl alcohol, it is essential to clean the underarm area thoroughly with soap and water. This will help to remove any sweat, bacteria, or dirt that may be present on the skin.

Dry the Underarm Area

After cleaning the underarm area, use a clean towel to dry the skin thoroughly. It is important to ensure that the skin is completely dry before applying the isopropyl alcohol.

Apply Isopropyl Alcohol

Take a small amount of isopropyl alcohol and apply it directly to the underarm area. You can use a cotton ball or a clean cloth to apply the alcohol.

Allow the Alcohol to Dry

Once the isopropyl alcohol is applied, allow it to dry completely before putting on clothes. This will ensure that the alcohol has enough time to kill the bacteria present on the skin.

Reapply As Necessary

Depending on the severity of the body odor, you may need to reapply the isopropyl alcohol throughout the day to keep the odor at bay.

It is important to note that isopropyl alcohol should not be applied to broken skin or areas with cuts, as it can be painful and cause irritation. Additionally, if the body odor persists even after applying isopropyl alcohol, it may be necessary to consult a medical professional for further evaluation.

Use Organic Coconut Oil

Organic coconut oil is a natural alternative to isopropyl alcohol and can be used to eliminate body odor that emanates from the armpits of a man. Here's how to apply organic coconut oil to get rid of underarm odor:

- Choose a high-quality organic coconut oil. Look for virgin or extra-virgin coconut oil, as these types are minimally processed and contain no additives.

- Take a small amount of the coconut oil and rub it between your palms to warm it up and make it easier to apply.

- Apply the coconut oil to your underarms, making sure to cover the entire area. Use enough coconut oil to ensure that your underarms are well moisturized.

- Be patient for the coconut oil to soak into your skin. It may take some minutes, but a bit of patience is required.

- Once the coconut oil has absorbed into your skin, put on a clean shirt. Avoid wearing tight-fitting clothing that may trap moisture and contribute to underarm odor.

- Repeat this process daily, preferably after showering, to maintain odor-free underarms.

Organic coconut oil works to eliminate underarm odor because it contains lauric acid, a fatty acid that has natural antimicrobial properties. This means that it can kill the bacteria that cause underarm odor without causing irritation or dryness. In addition to using organic coconut oil to eliminate underarm odor, it's important to maintain good hygiene practices. Shower daily, wear clean clothing, and use antibacterial soap or body wash to keep your skin clean and healthy.

Overall, for those who do not like chemicals in their body, organic coconut oil is a natural and effective alternative to isopropyl alcohol for eliminating underarm odor in men.

Fecal body odor is a distinct smell that resembles feces and can be caused by various factors. One possible cause is a poor diet, particularly one low in fiber, which can result in constipation and the inefficient processing of waste. When waste cannot be properly eliminated, toxins can be released back into the bloodstream, leading to an unpleasant odor.

Another potential cause of fecal body odor is a condition known as irritable bowel syndrome (IBS). Individuals with IBS may experience constant abdominal pain, as well as bouts of constipation or diarrhea. While the exact cause of IBS is still unknown, it is believed to be linked to sensitivity to certain foods or stress. Managing IBS symptoms often involves dietary adjustments, exercise, and medication.

Leaky gut syndrome is another condition that can contribute to fecal body odor. It occurs when the intestinal lining becomes damaged, leading to gastrointestinal issues such as bloating, food sensitivities, cramps, and excessive gas.

Trimethylaminuria (TMAU) is a rare metabolic disorder that affects the body's ability to process trimethylamine, a compound found in certain foods.

While the odor associated with TMAU may not always resemble feces, some individuals with this condition may experience a similar smell. Testing for TMAU can be an option for those who suspect it is the cause of their fecal body odor.

In summary, fecal body odor can result from factors such as a poor diet, irritable bowel syndrome, leaky gut syndrome, or, in rare cases, trimethylaminuria. Identifying and addressing the underlying cause can help manage this unpleasant symptom.

The information in this book has been presented in easy-to-understand simple language. It is intended to help you care for your hygiene as a man and eliminate body and foot odor. Should you have more questions that pertain to the tips provided in this book, you can email your questions to vayrious@gmail.com with the message title "The Men's Hygiene Handbook" and you shall receive a response.

Made in United States
Troutdale, OR
03/03/2025